CELTIC
TATTOOS

CELTIC TATTOOS

AILEEN MARRON

Quick, safe and temporary tattoos
from natural JAGUA paint

EDDISON•SADD EDITIONS

This book is dedicated to the Ancient Celts, Picts,
Scots and Britons, who left us a legacy of such
awe-inspiring artwork that we will be forever
striving to achieve such standards.

© 2007 by Eddison Sadd Editions

This 2007 edition published by Barnes & Noble, Inc. by arrangement with
Eddison Sadd Editions.

Text copyright © Aileen Marron 2007
Photographs copyright © Laura Knox, Peter Finley and Tony Finley 2007
Line illustrations copyright © Aileen Marron 2007

2007 Barnes & Noble

ISBN-13: 978-0-7607-9300-8
ISBN-10: 0-7607-9300-X

Eddison Sadd Editions Limited
St Chad's House, 148 King's Cross Road
London WC1X 9DH

Printed and bound in China

1 3 5 7 9 10 8 6 4 2

Contents

Introducing Celtic Tattoos

Celtic art has long since fascinated body artists and enthusiasts. The interlocking geometric spirals and key patterns are truly magical, and the interlacing knotwork and zoomorphic (animal-based) designs look like the creation of some greater power. These four main areas of Celtic design originate from the Pictish School of Celtic Art, the foundation for all artwork now commonly labelled as 'Celtic'. Early Celtic spiral patterns date back to the late Stone Age, peaking in the Dark Ages – the golden era for Celtic art – after the fall of Roman Britain.

Tattooing with woad
The ancient Britons – specifically the Picts who fought back the Roman advancement on today's Scotland – are believed to have tattooed or painted themselves with woad (a plant that yields a blue dye). This has not been proven; however, it is plausible that some of our British ancestors used woad to temporarily adorn their skin for battle or special occasions. Woad will only stain the skin for a couple of days, and the process is complex and time consuming; the traditional method used for textile colouring involved soaking the plant in urine!

Modern methods
Thankfully, there are now simpler ways to decorate our skin. There are permanent tattoo inks and temporary body-art dyes that are perfectly safe. Jagua products are ideally suited to temporary Celtic body art; the stain is long-lasting (10–15 days) and the colour range can perfectly reproduce many of the permanent black and grey Celtic designs that are popular today.

Above left Collecting the jagua fruit once they have been cut from the tree.

Above right Selecting the perfect jagua fruit for body art. The dark lines inside the fruit indicate a high genipine content.

What is a jagua tattoo?

Jagua can be found in Central and South America. It is the fruit of the jagua tree, the Latin name for which is *Genipa americana*. The fruit used to manufacture the paint used to create the designs shown in this book originates in the Chocó rainforest of Colombia, where it is called 'Jagua' (pronounced 'Hagua'). The fruit is known by different names in different regions – 'Jenipapo' in Brazil; 'Huito' in Peru. The unripe jagua fruit contains a natural and safe dye that works on the skin in just the same way as natural brown henna. The only difference is that jagua is black. Like henna, jagua has been used to create traditional body art for as long as anyone can remember.

Above left Grating the hard fruit: making jagua paint the traditional Emberra way.

Above right Beautiful Emberra jagua body art: this facial design is very popular in the rainforest.

Jagua – safe and natural

Jagua tattoos can now make their way into the spotlight, and our youth culture, much as henna did in the early 1990s. Hopefully, this will see an end to the unknowing and uncaring vendors often found working in tourist resorts, applying mislabelled and dangerous 'Black Henna Tattoos'. Body art created under this title is very likely to contain a chemical called para-phenylendiamine, which is illegal to use as a cosmetic ingredient in most countries that have legislation governing such products. This chemical is dangerous and should be avoided at all costs. Useful website addresses where you can find out more about the safety of temporary tattoos are given on page 78.

Part One
Creating Celtic Tattoos

In Part One I will show you everything you need to know to create your first Celtic tattoo. We'll cover the basic skills needed to use jagua products, and I will also provide some Celtic-specific advice for stress-free tattoo design and application. If you follow the instructions carefully, you'll soon be creating great Celtic tattoos every time!

Once you have chosen a design, you will learn how to make a transfer and transform it into a great Celtic tattoo. Painting with jagua couldn't be easier. The basic techniques are clearly illustrated, and as soon as you've mastered them you can get started.

Once you're comfortable with these straightforward techniques, I will teach you some more advanced skills that will enable you to really bring your tattoo to life. There are some great shading effects you can try, and we will also explore the fine-line techniques needed for some of the interlaced Celtic tattoo designs. If you're feeling inspired by Celtic design and are lured into its mazes and spirals, you may even venture into some freehand Celtic body art. You can begin by customizing some existing designs, and then gradually try out more ambitious and creative projects as you become more familiar with the construction of Celtic patterns.

Basic Skills

The prospect of re-creating any form of Celtic artwork can seem quite daunting to begin with, especially in the case of body art, where your canvas is neither flat nor motionless. The most important thing to remember is to work within your comfort zone, beginning with some of the simpler Celtic styles, and moving on to the more complex, multi-tonal interlacing designs once you have gained confidence. In this section we will cover the most basic skills, those that you need to create truly professional-looking Celtic tattoos right from the first attempt.

Design inspiration

Choosing a design can be surprisingly challenging; there are so many beautiful styles of Celtic artwork, all of which lend themselves to body art. To get you started I have created a selection of Celtic designs of different styles. These are shown on pages 13 to 23 and are ready for you to start creating transfers. All you have to do is decide which one to try first, and where on the body to place it. I suggest that you start with one of the simpler designs using one shade and no line work. I also advise you to choose an easy part of the body: the lower leg, ankle or foot if you're working on yourself; the upper arm, shoulder or back if you're working on a friend.

To help you choose a design, have a look at Part Two: Celtic Tattoo Gallery, to see how each design looks when it's completed. Once you've made your decision, turn to page 24 and we'll get started.

Working with transfers

Once you have chosen a design, you are ready to make a transfer. If you use the professional tools of the trade, this couldn't be easier. Tattoo design transfers, often called stencils, are one of the professional body artist's best-kept secrets. Transfers enable us to guarantee the final result of the artwork for the client. This is essential when working with many of the Celtic design styles, as well as precise work like lettering and logos where there is no room for artistic licence.

In the jagua tattoo industry, transfers are created using two key methods: one involves the use of a hectographic pencil and tracing paper; the other uses hectographic carbon paper. We will be using the first method here, as it enables us to create the most transfers. Hectographic pencils are particularly long-lasting, and can be used with any type of tracing paper to make transfers; however, for the best results, I do recommend that you use the thinnest tracing paper you can find.

1 Place your chosen design on a flat surface. Use a photocopy if you don't want to risk leaving pressure marks on the original artwork. If you're working on a wooden desk or table, put some paper underneath your design to avoid marking the wood.

4 Make sure the area of the body where you will be applying the tattoo is clean and free from moisturizers, sunscreens and other products. Then use a wet wipe or a thin layer of very soapy water to moisten the area.

2 Place the tracing paper on top of the design, holding it in position as you trace over the outline with a pen or pencil. You don't need to press very hard at this stage; the tracing just has to be clear enough to show through the tracing paper.

3 Turn the tracing paper over and place it on a sheet of plain paper. Use your hectographic pencil to trace over the outline of the design again, this time pressing firmly. Cut out the transfer so it is ready to use.

5 Press your transfer – hectographic pencil-side down – onto the moistened skin. Hold it firmly in place and tap it gently to make sure that the entire design makes contact with the skin. Take care not to allow the print to smudge.

6 Lift the transfer edge to check that it has printed on the skin, then carefully peel it away. If the print is too pale, this may be because: the transfer was pressed down too lightly; the skin is too dry; you didn't press hard enough with the hectographic pencil.

Paint application techniques

Jagua is available in a number of different formats, the most popular being gel and paint. Jagua gel is thicker than paint, and is ideal for line work and one-coat application. It can be applied straight from the tube. Simply cut open the nozzle and squeeze the tube as you draw. For finer detail and more delicate artwork, you can apply the gel using an application cone, holding it as you would if you were icing a cake. In this book we will be using jagua tattoo paint. This versatile product allows you to create different shades of black and grey – perfect for a lot of Celtic tattoo designs.

Using a selection of brushes and other application tools allows you to create many different tattoo effects.

Like all jagua tattoo products, the paint goes through a natural oxidization process when exposed to air, which enables it to dye the skin. It is therefore vital that you keep the bottle cap tightly closed when the paint is not in use. If oxidization starts to occur when the paint is in the bottle, there won't be as much of the process available to work when it is on the skin! When using a large bottle, professionals pour out a little at a time, keeping the bottle airtight to preserve the natural staining properties in the remainder of the paint. Remember that jagua is a permanent stain, so although it fades away on the skin, it won't come out of clothing, carpet, soft furnishings or untreated wood.

1 This brush is ideal for use by beginners. It has a small, fine tip, making it relatively easy to create sharp points and small designs.

2 To achieve a really good depth of colour you need to load your brush well. It may seem like a lot of paint to use at once, but it's quite thick so it won't drip or run.

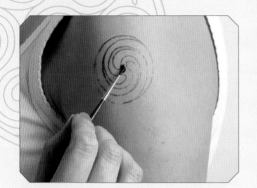

3 Touch down at one of the finer points or more intricate areas of a design, as it's useful to get a good quantity of paint into the smallest areas first. It's harder to go back and add extra paint later.

4 Work your brush back into the spirals. Lower the heel of the brush as you go, to release the rest of the paint. You're really using the brush to drag the thick paint along.

5 Add the second coat of paint liberally, allowing it to 'pool'. Use the tip of the brush to literally pull the paint along the thinner lines of the design.

6 Check for holes (sometimes caused by air bubbles) and transparent patches. Add more paint where necessary, using the tip of the brush to manipulate it into the thinner areas.

Creating a Celtic jagua tattoo

Now that you've learned the basic painting technique and had some practice at making and applying transfers, you're ready to create your first Celtic jagua tattoo. I have chosen a bold and beautiful triskele design that I based on a spiral group from *The Book Of Durrow*. This Celtic style is easy to achieve. Nevertheless, it is beautiful to behold and the magical allure of the Celtic triskele design draws you in to its never-ending spirals. The contrast of the jagua stain against the colour of the skin makes for a stunning Celtic tattoo.

I have chosen to apply this tattoo to the upper arm. This is a great area of the body to work on first, as well as being one of the more popular areas on which people choose to have both permanent and temporary tattoos. When working on this area, it's very easy for both you and your friend to sit comfortably, allowing your 'canvas' to relax, and therefore stay relatively still. Likewise, you will be able to con-centrate on the design rather than on aches and pains caused by sit-ting awkwardly. Ideally, rest your friend's arm on an armrest or your knees so that their forearm is at 90 degrees to their upper arm. When you're both ready, follow the step-by-step instructions that follow, using the photographs to guide you.

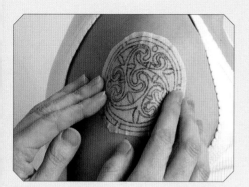

1 Moisten the skin with a wet wipe and press the transfer, face down, onto the skin. Press firmly to make sure that the whole design makes contact with the skin.

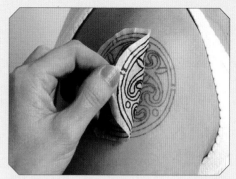

2 Carefully peel away the transfer, revealing the outline of the design left behind on the skin.

3 Begin to paint the tattoo, starting at the top and working down, to avoid smudging. Load your brush well and apply the paint as heavily as you can.

4 To ensure a strong black colour, apply a second coat of paint straight away. To achieve the best results, make sure there are no transparent areas.

5 When finished, the design should have a solid shiny black coating of jagua paint that is visibly raised off the skin. Take care not to smudge it while you wait for the paint to dry.

6 The paint takes between 20 minutes and 1 hour to dry, depending on the size of the design and the temperature and humidity of the surroundings. Once the paint is dry, the tattoo will look dull and flat.

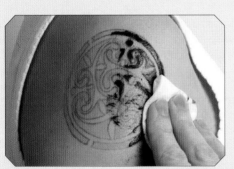

7 The paint must be left on for a full 2 hours for the jagua stain to take full effect. Then simply rinse off the paint in cool water (don't use soap) and pat dry. Alternatively, remove the paint using some damp paper towels.

8 At first, the colour of your jagua tattoo will be so pale that you may not even see it. It will develop through bluey-grey tones over the next 12–48 hours. The final colour varies greatly from one individual to another, but it will be dark grey or black.

How does jagua work?

The oxidization process

Jagua body-art products contain a botanical stain that occurs naturally in unripe jagua fruit. The active staining compound is called genipine, and this natural colour works to stain the skin in much the same way as lawsone does in henna products.

This photograph shows an unripe jagua fruit that has been cut in half. The instant the fruit was sliced into, the genipine started the oxidization process and began to darken itself and the entire centre of the fruit. In the few moments between cutting the fruit and the photograph being taken, the seeds and the surrounding tissue had already begun to turn from pure white to creamy brown.

Above The oxidization process begins as soon as the jagua fruit is cut open.

Below After one day, the entire centre of the fruit is black.

The next photograph shows the same fruit just twenty-four hours later. You can clearly see the results of the oxidization process: the genipine compound has stained the entire centre of the fruit. It has achieved this intense colour because the genepine is concentrated inside the relatively small fruit, and is in its most active state.

On the skin

The skin is composed of three basic layers: fatty tissue in the hypo-
dermis, the dermis and the epidermis. The epidermis is the outermost
layer of the skin and is in a constant state of renewal. The basal layer
of the epidermis continually creates new cells. These cells rise up to
the surface where they eventually die and are shed, only to be
replaced by newer cells as they, too, push forward towards the surface.
It is the layers of dead cells at the uppermost part of the epidermis
that jagua stains.

The renewal process takes between one and four weeks, the average
being two to three weeks, depending on the area of the body, the
health of the skin and external factors like severe cold and wind chill
or intense heat and humidity. Where there are more layers of dead
cells, the jagua has more layers to stain so the intensity of the colour
will be deeper. However, this is less noticeable with jagua than with
henna because a jagua stain is black whereas henna is brown.

As the body sheds its skin and new cells rise to the surface, the jagua
tattoo will gradually fade through tones of grey until it completely
disappears. The jagua tattoo product contained in this kit has been
specially formulated so it doesn't stain your body hair, meaning that
once your tattoo fades away you won't be left with dyed-black hairs.
Do be careful with your nails, however, as the product will stain them
if they come into contact with one another and you will have to wait
for the colour to grow out.

Making the most of your jagua tattoo

Jagua tattoos eventually disappear, and therein lies the beauty – you can change the design, size and position of your tattoo as often as you like. But, you will probably want it to last as long as possible. Follow these useful tips to get the best from your jagua tattoo.

- Before you begin, exfoliate, cleanse and dry the skin to remove any grease.
- Leave the jagua on the skin for 2 hours, even if it is dry after 1 hour.
- Rinse the area with cool water to remove the paint. Don't use soap or hot water.
- Keep the tattoo moisturized, making sure the product is well absorbed before covering the tattoo with clothing.
- Try not to allow your clothes to rub the tattoo too much.
- Avoid saunas, hot tubs and chlorinated water. If you do go swimming, cover the tattoo with a water-repellent barrier; try cocoa butter or a beeswax-based lip balm.
- Avoid contact with harsh chemicals. If you have jagua on your hands, wear rubber gloves when washing up or cleaning.

Ten days after its creation, this jagua tattoo is fading away. It will disappear completely in the coming week.

Advanced Skills

Now that you've mastered the basics you can move on to more adventurous projects. In this section we'll aim to advance your entire skill base, from the designs you choose to work from, through to the techniques you use. You will learn the skills needed to create all kinds of Celtic tattoos: shading techniques that are used for the ornate zoomorphic (animal-based) designs; line work, essential for some of the more intricate Celtic styles such as interlacing knotwork and key-pattern designs. And, to top it all off, we'll tackle freehand artwork, a real challenge in the Celtic arena! Once you start to become more adventurous, there'll be no stopping you. You never know – you might start out customizing a few Celtic knots and finish up designing full back pieces!

Fine line work using jagua gel is here combined with jagua-paint shading to amazing effect.

Customizing designs

Customizing existing patterns is one of the best ways to advance your tattoo-designing skills. This is especially relevant to Celtic styles, as designing brand-new Celtic tattoos can be intimidating even to the most accomplished artist. When you first try your hand at customizing, take a small section of a Celtic design – a knot or a triskele, perhaps – and use it to form the basis of an entirely different piece: for example, use it repeatedly to form an ankle bracelet or an armband. Alternatively, use the detail as a centrepiece in a much larger design: a Celtic mandala, for instance, building the design outwards from the middle. You could replace some of the triskeles in a band with your own unique designs, or add tendrils and fruit to a 'Tree of life' design. You could even try embellishing a design with some of

The basic triskele design (*see page 28*) is used as a centrepiece in a much more complex Celtic mandala.

the spiral patterns shown in the Basic Skills section – create some large line-work shapes, then fill them with spirals.

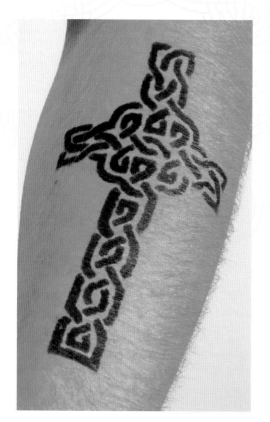

You may choose to plan your alterations before you start, then make a transfer that includes your customization – well-planned artwork makes for smooth and stress-free application. This is a very wise approach for most complex Celtic tattoo designs. It's very difficult to create accurate multi-lace knots totally freehand. Or, you may make changes to a design as you go along. Although daunting at first, this approach can be quite liberating, allowing you to use the basis of one Celtic design to create your own unique version. You can get some really great results this way as you will be taking the body's natural contours into account.

The Celtic cross

The Celtic cross is a very popular design in today's western body art culture, even though the origins of the design go back

Left Positive Celtic cross

to before the Dark Ages! The two Celtic crosses shown here look quite different; however, they are derived from the same transfer outline (*see page 21*).

For the version shown left, I filled in the knotwork with jagua to create a 'positive' effect. The result is a very bold design that uses the skin tone as a contrasting background for the dark jagua.

The Celtic cross shown on the right is a 'negative' form that gives it a totally different look, but which is equally effective. I applied the jagua in the negative spaces created by the transfer outline. I chose to use gel rather than paint for this version in order to apply very thin lines around the Celtic knotwork. Then I outlined the entire shape of the cross. To complete the design, I filled in the tiny spaces left between the sets of fine line work. The resulting tattoo uses the dark jagua colour as the background and the skin tone creates the knotwork itself.

Right Negative Celtic cross

Working freehand

As you become more confident with customizing Celtic designs, you may find that you are drawn towards freehand techniques, or even that you start creating designs from scratch. The instructions and illustrations shown over the next few pages will help to increase your confidence, giving you the freedom to concentrate on the weaving construction and maze-like complexity of Celtic design.

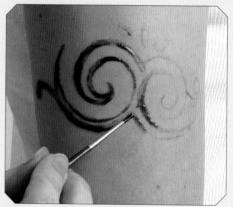

1 Using your paintbrush, mark out the areas of your design that you will be working on first. You can do this using a really thin coat of jagua paint or by visualizing where you will need to paint and placing little guides to lead the way – whichever works best for you. Always try to think ahead a little as you plan out your creation.

2 Now follow your guides. At this stage you can work out any problems, smoothing out curves and straightening edges as you go. Start from a point at the top left of your design and work your brush backwards towards the right (or from right to left if you are left-handed) using the techniques that you have learned.

If Celtic knotwork is too complicated to attempt just yet but you still want to work freehand, try exploring some ancient spiral patterns, such as those shown below. This way you can explore the realms of freehand artwork along with continuous free-flowing Celtic spirals without getting tied up in knots!

3 Once you are happy with your freehand outline, you can start to fill in your design in the same way as if you were filling in a transfer image. Remember to load your brush well and to work the paint into all of the areas of the design, literally pulling it into the tighter spaces.

4 When you've completed one layer, if you want a really deep colour, thickly apply a second coat. If you prefer a charcoal-grey tone, allow the jagua to dry as it is. After two hours, remove the paint with cool water and wait for your freehand tattoo to develop.

Using guides

Freehand Celtic designs are a challenge. To help you, mark out some guides before you start to apply the jagua paint. Try out the following techniques and see what works for you.

1 Use an eyebrow pencil to roughly sketch a simple Celtic knot.   *2* Jagua paint can then be applied with confidence.

Apply guides using a liquid eyeliner or a soft eyebrow pencil. These lines aren't supposed to be perfect, nor do they need to be in exactly the same place as your final tattoo. Just apply them quickly to help make sure that your knots end up where you want them and to maintain the general size and shape of your design. You can also sketch out complicated knots in this way to create a foundation on which you can build with your jagua.

The process of creating freehand designs such as armbands and ankle bracelets can be simplified by defining your working area. You can do this using guides, as described on the previous page, but a quicker, more effective, technique is to mask out the area using a low-tack tape such as surgical tape. This method allows you to form the outline for Celtic bands and for larger, more complex, tattoos in no time. Once the area is masked, you can clearly see where you need to work, making your freehand artwork more accurate. You can also combine the techniques, using additional guides within your masked-out areas. If you wish, you can leave the tape in place until you have applied the jagua and left it to dry.

1 Surgical tape is quick to apply and creates a clear working space.

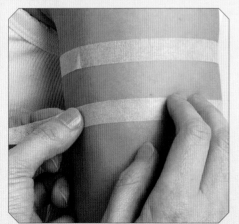

2 When the working space is defined, a simple knotwork band can quickly be marked out using guides.

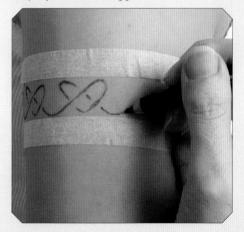

Celtic shading techniques

Jagua is perfect for creating temporary Celtic body art. Its long-lasting natural colouring properties make it possible to create and wear designs that closely resemble permanent Celtic tattoos. This is particularly apparent with black and grey shaded designs. By replicating the effect of a permanent tattoo with jagua paint, we are able to create some truly exquisite artwork.

By altering the thickness of the paint you will determine the final shade of the jagua stain. There are a number of ways to achieve this. You can apply different shades in one stroke, by using a flick of the wrist to adjust the thickness of the paint. This technique is ideal for adding shadow to a design. Another method involves building up shades of grey using thin layers of paint, as illustrated below.

Here you can see the full range of shades that you can achieve. The lightest shade uses one layer of paint; the darkest uses four. The colour of the paint on the skin will be similar to the colour of the finished jagua tattoo.

Turn to page 49 to see the final result that can be achieved when shading techniques are incorporated into a Celtic tattoo design.

Celtic line work

A lot of Celtic tattoos require very fine line artwork: for example, the interlaced-knotwork ankle bracelet shown on page 52. It is possible to create fine lines with jagua paint, but for truly delicate designs it is much more practical to use jagua tattoo gel. You can apply the gel straight from a tube (see below) or, for even finer detail, through an application cone – as you would if you were working with henna paste. For details on where to source jagua tattoo gel, turn to the Useful Addresses section on page 78.

Cut off the end of the tube nozzle to release the jagua gel. To create finer lines for more delicate artwork, carefully pierce the end of the nozzle with a pin to make a smaller opening. Then simply hold the tube like a pen and squeeze gently as you go along to release a fine line of jagua gel.

Creating more advanced Celtic tattoos

We've looked at both simple and intricate designs. You've learned how to adapt designs and how to create transfers for some stunning Celtic styles. You've developed freehand skills and tried your hand at shading and line work techniques. You are probably beginning to understand the principles and the basic methods of construction that form the building blocks of Celtic design. Put all this together and you will be

1 After applying the transfer outline, start working with the jagua gel from the top left corner of the design (top right if you're left handed). To create lines as thin as those shown here, it is advisable to use a tube of jagua gel with the end pierced, or a fine-line application cone.

2 Work slowly and cautiously with the gel to avoid creating blobs in the corners or where two lines meet. The most challenging areas are the knotwork lines and the hind legs.

well on the way to creating beautiful, ornate Celtic tattoos such as the zoomorphic (animal-based) design illustrated below.

The step-by-step instructions in this sequence demonstrate how to create a complex Celtic design using all the basic and advanced skill sets that you have come across in this book. This design uses both jagua paint and gel, and incorporates shading and fine-line techniques, with a few freehand additions to finish it off.

3 Allow the gel to dry a little before you start to add the paint; 20 minutes is usually sufficient. First apply the paint to the areas where you want the lightest shades. You can apply it in very thin coats, or, as I have done here, fairly liberally. This level of coverage will create a light-grey tone on the skin.

4 Apply more paint to any areas where you wish to create a darker grey tone. Again, you can build up these shades using very thin layers, or, as I have done here, liberally apply paint, working it into the thinner undercoat and blending it in with your brush.

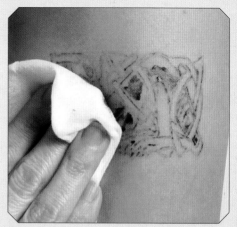

5 Leave the jagua on the skin for two hours. Once it is dry, peel away the gel and any paint that comes off with it. This can be tricky on hairy areas!

6 Once most of the dried gel has been removed, gently wash off the paint using cool water or damp paper towels. Do not try to wash off the outlines from your transfer at this point, or you may hinder the development of the tattoo. When all the jagua has been removed, pat the area dry and wait for the tattoo to develop.

I hope you have enjoyed both the basic and advanced guidance given here to get you started on the path to becoming a Celtic body artist. Whether you are developing your skills in order to have fun with your friends and family, or in order to build a career as a professional body artist, just remember to have fun with jagua and your Celtic artwork. After all, it wears off in a few weeks, so the cycle can begin again in a truly Celtic fashion!

Part Two

Celtic Tattoo Gallery

The body art shown in the gallery was created using the techniques covered in Part One. Some of the tattoos involve making and using design transfers; some have been customized after transfer application; others are totally freehand and have been created as I work.

These jagua tattoos were photographed two days after application, so they have had a chance to develop to their optimum colour. You'll notice that the colour of the jagua varies from one person to another. The same product was applied to all four models and was left to develop on the skin for two hours in each case. This perfectly illustrates the true nature of a jagua tattoo: the skin type will determine the ultimate colour. Skin tone has nothing to do with the final shade – sometimes the darkest colour is achieved on the palest skin tones, and sometimes on the darkest. Once you have tried jagua, you will know the range of shades that you are able to achieve on your own skin. As a general rule it will also go darkest on the hands and feet, where the epidermis is thickest.

The gallery can serve a number of purposes. Some of the photographs show how the designs given in Part One should look when finished, so you may find these useful when you're trying them out for the first time. When you're a little more advanced, use the gallery for inspiration – every tattoo is totally achievable and will help to get you on your way to creating Celtic designs of your own.

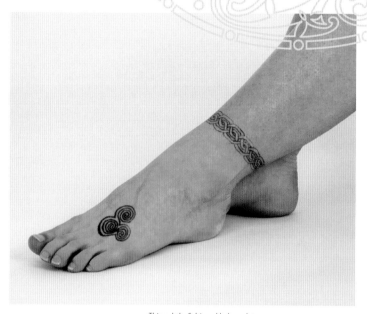

This subtle Celtic ankle bracelet
involves very fine lines and has been
created using jagua gel. The design
on Philippa's foot is inspired by
ancient stone carvings found at
Newgrange in Ireland.

Michelle's back piece is a combination of freehand artwork and transfer designs. I used three triskele design transfers and applied the rest of the piece by hand.

◀ You can see several of Jack's tattoos here. I love the bold spiral-inspired design on his upper arm, peeking out from behind his T-shirt!

▶ Jo's jagua paint is almost dry, but she still has another hour to wait before it is removed.

◄ Philippa is obviously enjoying her Celtic tattoos!

▶ This triskele mandala has turned out beautifully. It's a shame that Santiago won't be able to see it without the aid of mirrors . . .

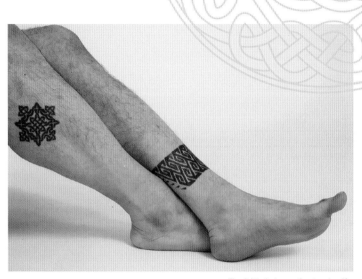

The Celtic design on Santiago's calf has a distinctly Moroccan feel to it, and the key-pattern design on his ankle is really effective.

As you can see here, I love triskele designs. It's a good thing that Philippa likes them too – the spiral patterns really suit her!

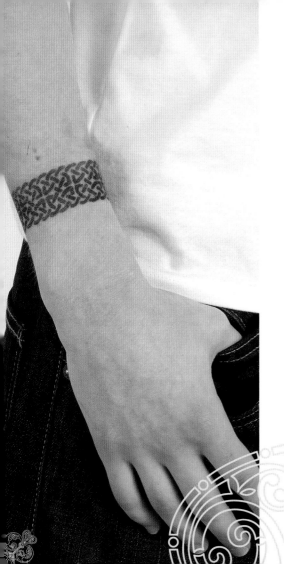

◀ The tight knotwork on this bracelet really works. It is intricate and detailed, yet very masculine.

▲ Here, you can clearly see the effects that can be achieved when you incorporate shading and line work. I used Jack's skin tone to show the line work in this Celtic mandala.

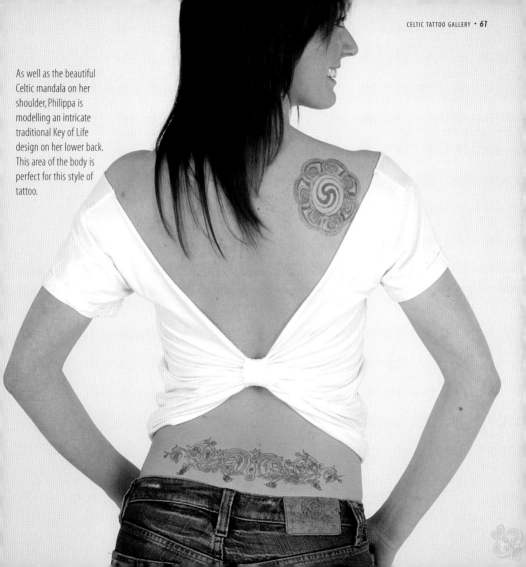

As well as the beautiful Celtic mandala on her shoulder, Philippa is modelling an intricate traditional Key of Life design on her lower back. This area of the body is perfect for this style of tattoo.

◀ I think it is safe to say that all the models liked their Celtic tattoos!

Jack's spiral-inspired upper-arm tattoo in more detail. The negative space adds as much to the design as the jagua itself.

Celtic triskeles are definitely in! Both models are displaying triskele armbands; Phillippa's is very elegant and Santiago's is more masculine.

A close-up of Santiago's armband clearly shows the construction of the design.

Jo and Jack: Jo's tattoos are still drying in this photo, but you can see how the zoomorphic tattoo will turn out by just looking at the shading in the wet paint.

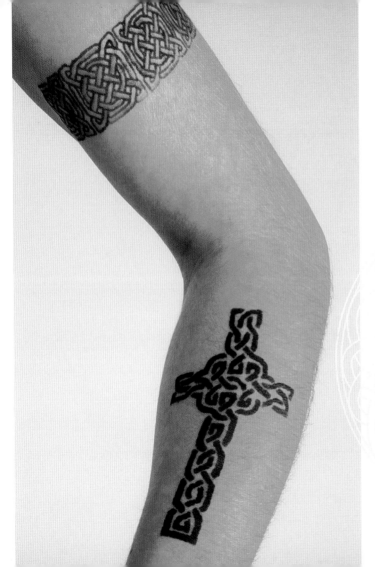

Jack's Celtic cross looks stunning! I also love the softness of the armband. I used jagua gel for the line work, then added a little paint to the knotwork to make it stand out against Jack's skin tone.

Part Three

The Celts and Body Art

Omnes vero se Britanni vitro inficiunt, quod caeruleum efficit colorem …

'The whole truth is the Britons dye themselves with woad because it makes their complexions blue…'

JULIUS CAESAR, *The Gallic Wars: The Conquest of Gaul*

Across the globe our ancestors used various pigments and stains to colour and mark their skin. Ultimately, body art is a very important aspect of aboriginal life, often overlooked by archaeologists and historians because of the lack of physical evidence, which, due to its very nature, is very hard to come by. So when researching civilizations that have effectively died out, we are left with only a few records and tales and, very occasionally, a tiny piece of physical evidence to draw our conclusions by. I will offer some examples here.

Contrary to popular belief, the Celts did not originate from Scotland. In fact, they first formed as a distinct group around 1,000 BCE, close to the borders of eastern France, northern Switzerland and south-west Germany. Over the next five thousand years the Celts spread far and wide, through France and Spain, as far south as Italy and across to the British Isles. The rise of the continental Celts peaked in 390 BCE, before they disintegrated under Roman impact. From the sixth century CE, the Celtic language was heard only in the British Isles.

This cloth has been dyed using woad. When the cloth is lifted out of the mixture, it turns from yellow to green and, finally, to blue when it oxidizes in the air.

Using woad

The Celts of Britain occupied most regions of England and Wales, and those living in the north were often at war with their Scottish counterparts, the Picts. The first reference to Celtic body art dates back to early Roman Britain. The quotation shown on page 69 is taken from Caesar's description of the Celtic people of Kent in south-east England, at the time of the Roman invasion. It is one of the few passages that records the use of Celtic body art using the temporary bluish stain from woad, which resulted in a terrifying appearance useful in battle. Some historians claim that the word 'vitro' in this phrase, could have meant 'glass', but I agree with the Latin scholars that Caesar was referring to woad, which was widely used for the dyeing of textiles at that time. Most villages would have had at least one woad vat in use. In the likely event that our ancestors painted themselves with this dye, the liquid would oxidize on the skin and develop into a temporary bluish stain that lasted for a couple of days.

Copper pigments

In 1984, the body of an Iron Age man known as Lindow Man (locally known as Pete because he was recovered from a peat bog) was discovered at Lindow Moss in Cheshire, north-west England. This fascinating find provided physical evidence to suggest that some two thousand years ago the Celts of Cheshire created effective permanent tattoos using copper pigments. These pigments could also be used to make body paints by preparing with rendered fat and spreading the concoction onto the surface of the skin, in much the same way as we may use grease paints today – only more toxic; we now know that copper pigments should not be used on the skin.

The Picts

The Picts were the ancestral tribes of Northern Britain (today's Scotland), and, when we speak of Celts today, it is usually Picts that we are referring to. There is much debate about whether the Picts were of Celtic origin or were in fact the first inhabitants of Scotland. Either way, it is agreed that the Picts were true masters of Celtic artwork. During the time of the Picts, and the following era of the Picts and the Scots (the first Scots migrated from Northern Ireland), Celtic artwork developed to its greatest heights in both Scotland and Ireland.

The Romans' collective name for the Picts was *Pictii*, meaning 'painted ones'. This significantly reinforces the concept that the Picts, like the Celts, decorated their bodies in some way. The Irish called the Picts *Cruithne*, which is often translated as 'people of designs'. There is another translation that may stem from the root *Kwr*, meaning 'to cut'. Both theories could be taken to describe the Picts as tattooed.

It is unknown whether the Picts used woad to colour their skin; however, there is evidence to suggest that they did carry out permanent tattoo procedures. In the seventh century CE, the following statement was recorded by a Spanish bishop, Isadore of Seville:

> *'The race of the Picts has a name derived from the appearance of their bodies. These are played upon by a needle working with small pricks and by the squeezed-out sap of a native plant, so that they bear the resultant marks according to the personal rank of the individual, their painted limbs being tattooed to show their high birth.'*

We don't know exactly what kind of plant 'sap' may have been used – this could be an incorrect assumption; however, the description of the needle working over the skin is a definite reference to permanent tattooing.

In the fifth century CE, a Roman poet named Claudius Claudianus made two references to the practice of permanent tattooing by the Picts. In the first, he says:

'Dressed in the skin of a Caledonian beast, her cheeks tattooed, a sea-blue mantle sweeping over her footsteps like the surge of the ocean.'

It is debatable whether Claudius is describing a Pictish woman or drawing a comparison between a local woman and the land itself. What is unmistakable, though, is the reference to the woman's tattooed cheeks. In his second reference, Claudius says:

'The legion which had been left to guard far-distant Britain, which had kept the fierce Scots in check and gazed at the strange shapes tattooed on the faces of the dying Picts.'

Here, Claudius is talking about the Roman legion who guarded the borders of Roman Britain. He describes the bravery of the Roman soldiers fighting the Scots, and refers to the tattooed faces of the Pictish warriors. In both quotations, the word 'tattooed' is derived from the literal translation, 'iron marked', from the Latin, *ferro picta*, *ferro notatas*.

The changing role of body art

It is highly probable that, all over the British Isles, people decorated their bodies with permanent or temporary markings. It would certainly be in accordance with the worldwide tendency to embellish the skin for celebrations, rituals, religious ceremonies, rites of passage and even for warfare. The end of the widespread use of body art as a form of ritual can probably be attributed to the acceptance of Christianity in ancient Britain and Ireland. There are a number of references to ancient Christian tattoos being frowned upon by the church. In the late eighth century, Pope Hadrian 1 officially forbade all body art practices.

Tattoos today

I firmly believe that ancient civilizations from all around the world practised body art in one way or another. I would have to see solid evidence to the contrary if I am to be convinced that an ancient culture existed that did not practise such an intrinsic human behaviour. Even today, body art is thriving; permanent and temporary tattoos, body painting, face painting, piercing, make-up, nail polish and hair dye are all used to adorn the body, whether for special occasions, ceremonial events, daily use or just for fun. Even though the evidence supporting ancient Celtic body art may be considered sparse by some, I find it compelling and fascinating, and I hope that I have shed some light on our Celtic body art heritage.

Celtic art styles

I felt it would be useful to show you where I found the inspiration for the tattoo designs shown in Parts One and Two. So, here I wish to share with you the styles of Celtic artwork that were practised throughout ancient Britain and Ireland. Sadly, there are no accurate records of the Celtic body art styles used in ancient times. But, I'm sure their creations would have been equally as beautiful and spiritual as all the other Celtic artwork that has stood the test of time.

Many Celtic styles are literally constructed rather than drawn. It helps if you can visualize the designs in three dimensions. For the real Celtic artwork enthusiast, I recommend you buy George Bain's practical book, *Celtic Art: The Methods of Construction*. This is a treasure among books, and I am sure that every practising Celtic artist has a copy! Don't be put off by the intricacy of the Celtic styles; you can plan your own Celtic designs geometrically, then make transfers to help you apply them as jagua tattoos.

Prehistoric art

The triskele design shown here is taken directly from a stone in the inner chamber at Newgrange, a megalithic burial chamber in County Meath, Ireland. The burial chamber covers over an acre of land, and dates back approximately 5,500 years. The creators of this tomb are believed to be the first druids to use a solar calendar; to this day, the dawn sunrise on the Winter Solstice travels down the 62-foot entrance corridor to illuminate the central chamber, which is decorated with some of the earliest pagan Celtic designs.

The development of spirals

The spiral designs, like those first seen at Newgrange, are the most widespread form of Celtic art, crossing regions and timelines. The spirals are thought to represent divinity, and the triple spiral, known as the triskele, is the most spiritual of them all, representing the circle of life and death – the sun, the afterlife and reincarnation. It is also representative of the relationship between the earth, the water and the sky.

Key patterns

Key patterns are very well known in Greece, and it is often assumed that the Greeks passed on this artform to the Romans, who, in turn, brought it to Britain where the Celts picked up the influence. This is not the case. There are plenty of examples of pre-Roman Celtic art, not to mention Pictish art, where key patterns abound. The key patterns themselves can be approached as spiral patterns composed of either straight or diagonal lines. As shown on the Farr Stone (*see page 77*), key patterns can be used in conjunction with all other styles of Celtic design.

Above The Battersea Shield demonstrates that spirals were used for decoration as early as the Iron Age.

Interlacing knotwork construction

The interlacing knotwork borders and panels are probably the best-recognized style of Celtic design. The intricate weaving is mesmerizing, and the construction of these works illustrates an incredible command of geometry and mathematics. The most important aspect is the continuity of the interlacing knotwork (*see left*); there is no beginning and no end – it is a never-ending thread woven into a work of art. It is really important to maintain the 'over, under' weave throughout the construction, to achieve the right effect.

Animal and human design forms

The background of the designs based on animal forms (zoomorphic; *see below*) and human forms (anthropomorphic) comes directly from Christianity. The pre-Christian eras of Celtic art show no signs of zoomorphic designs. The earlier pagans did not directly copy aspects of life in their art; they were truly abstract in their creations. Perhaps this is why Celtic art styles are so highly developed compared to similar styles throughout the rest of the world. However, with the introduction of Christianity, it became acceptable to record creation. So,

images of plants, animals and humans became woven into the fabric of the Celtic interlacing knotwork style, most beautifully represented in some of the illustrated manuscripts, like *The Book of Lindisfarne* and *The Book of Kells*.

Christian-influenced Celtic design

The Celtic crosses shown on the right illustrate the Celtic artwork carved into stone by highly skilled masons. Both crosses are Class 3 Pictish Stones (they feature none of the ancient

Above left The Farr Stone.
Above A Celtic cross showing interlacing knotwork.

Pictish markings, only Christian symbolism). The Farr Stone dates back to the eighth or ninth century, and stands at Bettyhill at the northern tip of Scotland. It beautifully illustrates all the Celtic styles that we have looked at: knotwork, key patterns, spirals and zoomorphic designs. The second Celtic cross illustrates how the craft developed: the stone slab is no longer used as a tablet for artwork; instead, the cross is sculpted out of the stone. Only the interlacing knotwork style is used here.

Illustrated manuscripts

The highlight of the Christian-influenced Celtic period has to be the illustrated manuscripts, of which *The Book of Kells* is one example, beautifully illustrated by monks of incredible skill. It is also known as 'The Book of Columba', as it was started at the monastery at Iona, built by Columba, an irish Monk who settled in Scotland. The book was taken to Kells, in Ireland, to be completed safely, away from the Norse raiders who were present in Scotland at that time.

Above From *The Book of Kells*

Useful Addresses

Established in 1993, my company was the original manufacturer and supplier of retail and professional henna body art products. It now has two levels: Primal Cosmetics Ltd, a manufacturing company; and www.TraditionalBodyArt.com, a retail platform where you will find a whole host of invaluable products including the revolutionary jagua tattoo range and the professional henna body art range. To find your nearest jagua stockist and for further information about jagua products and the responsible manufacturing of our ranges, please contact Primal Cosmetics Ltd (see address below).

Primal Cosmetics Ltd

Unit 6, Tattenham Works, Leigh Road, Hindley Green, Lancashire, WN2 4SZ, UK

Tel: +44 (0)1942 255909
email: info@primalcosmetics.com
Website: www.primalcosmetics.com

www.jaguatattoos.com

A fully updated information resource website, complete with video demonstrations and articles. Email info@jaguatattoos.com

www.hennatattoos.com

A fully updated information resource website, complete with video demonstrations and articles. Email info@hennatattoos.com

www.thebodyartshop.com

A secure shopping site offering a huge range of safe, quality-assured body art products for international delivery.
Tel: 0845 257 3040 (UK – local rate)
Tel: +44 (0)161 408 3344 (International)
email: sales@thebodyartshop.com

www.thebodyartforums.com

An open-minded forum for the debate, discussion and development of different forms of body art, including natural henna and jagua.

www.JRCF.org.uk

The Jagua Rainforest Communities Fund (JRCF), a profit-sharing scheme where we work directly with the communities involved with the responsible harvesting of jagua for our products.
email admin@jrcf.org.uk

www.aileenmarron.co.uk

Visit my blog to learn more about my work.
email: aileen@aileenmarron.co.uk

About the Author

I have been working as a freelance body artist in the UK and overseas since 1993. Although I am experienced in a whole variety of temporary body art products, my specialist fields are henna and jagua. I spent my childhood and teenage years in Kuwait in the Middle East, where traditional Arabic floral henna designs captured my heart and my imagination. I returned to England in 1990 and started college in Manchester, where I met my long-term business partner (and husband), Simon Finley. We set up our first henna business in 1993. By 1997 we had a small business devoted to manufacturing temporary body art products, and were also running various training courses and artist venues. In addition, we launched our body art supply and support website, www.hennatattoos.com. 1998 saw the publication of my first book, *The Henna Body Art Book*, which is still in print today.

Ever since those early days we have been on an unstoppable quest to find the fabled safe, black and natural stain. We've been working on our jagua products since late 2004, and I am delighted that I've now been able to introduce you to jagua tattoos – another wonder of the rainforests of Latin America!

The project that we are involved with is one of the three projects supported by UNCTAD (United Nations Conference on Trade and Development), out of one hundred proposed projects. It is hoped that, in the near future, the responsible management and collection of jagua for the international cosmetics, food and textile industries will provide a sustainable source of income to a growing number of communities who live within the rainforests.

Acknowledgements

First of all I'd like to acknowledge my incredibly skilled Celtic ancestors for their amazing artwork legacy. No doubt anyone who attempts to replicate Celtic designs (never mind create new ones) will appreciate the technical brilliance of the original masters! As always, thanks to Simon for his support and patience while I've been writing this book. I'd also like to thank Simon, and Michelle Nicholson, for their help on 'Celtic jagua tattoo day' – I couldn't have got through all the designs without you. Thanks again to everyone at Eddison Sadd Editions, especially Elaine Partington and Katie Golsby. Thanks also to Pat and Keith Marron (Mum and Dad), Jeanette and Tony Finley and all the islanders for their continued support and hard work. Extra-special thanks to Dad, for helping me with the Latin, and to Peter and Tony Finley for taking photos in sub-zero temperatures in the Scottish Highlands in the middle of winter!

Eddison · Sadd Editions

Eddison Sadd Editions would like to thank the models who appear in this book: Joanna Beaufoy, Jack Hughes, Santiago Alcon and Philippa Messenger.

Picture credits: Picture Contact/Alamy 70; British Museum/Art Archive 75; Art Archive 77.

Editorial Director	Ian Jackson
Senior Editor	Katie Golsby
Proofreader	Peter Kirkham
Art Director	Elaine Partington
Line artwork	Anthony Duke
Picture research	Diana Morris
Production	Cara Herron